PRA

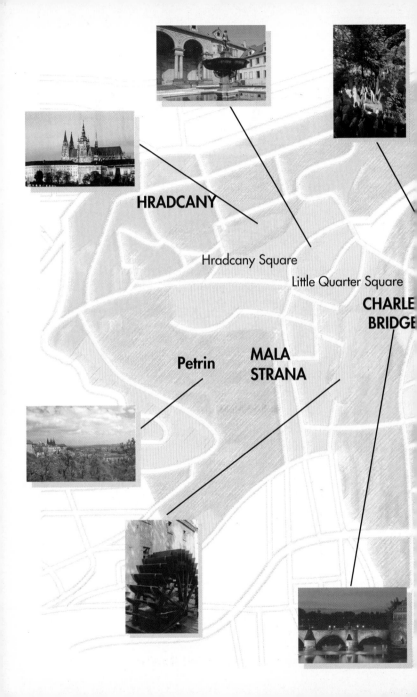

HRADCANY

Hradcany Square

Little Quarter Square

CHARLE
BRIDGE

Petrin

MALA
STRANA

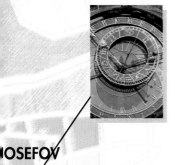

JOSEFOV

Old Town Square

STARE MESTO

Wenceslas Square

NOVE MESTO

Charles Square

0   500 m

A stone head in the Vysehrad cemetery. It was here in the ancient fortress of the Premyslids that Libuse had a vision of the future magnificence of Prague.

Once upon a time on the banks of the Vltava there lived a princess named Libuse who had a dream of building a great city...

The coat of arms of the Old Town.

The story of Prague

The city of Prague has stood at the crossroads of the routes crossing Europe from north to south and east to west for more than a thousand years. Not surprisingly, it abounds in culture. The river Vltava (or Moldau in German) flows through Prague and has always been its source of life. Situated at the heart of Bohemia, a region famous for its beer, crystal and delicious white wines, this city of a hundred towers is without doubt one of the most charming capitals in Europe. Whatever the season, there is always plenty to see and do!

The houses in Prague are often beautifully ornate.

Libuse dreamed of building a city of such importance and renown that foreign kings would bow down at its threshold, or praha in Czech. She founded a settlement for the Czech people at Prague and along with her husband, Premysl, founded the first Czech dynasty, known as the Premyslids.

Long ago, the Czech tribe settled on the rocky cliffs of Vysehrad where its leader, Princess Libuse, married Premysl. The choice of site for Libuse's fantastic city came to her in a dream and it was here in Praha (Prague) that the empire was destined to be built. Later, in the 10th century, during the reign of Wenceslas who later become the patron saint of the city, the Czech state expanded and went from strength to strength.

The city of Prague has many palaces. Most of them are found around the castle in the area known as Hradcany.

The baroque splendour of the Monastery of Our Lady of Loreto is an imposing reminder of the Catholic domination imposed on Prague by the Habsburgs.

The tram is a practical way of getting around the city.

Bohemia, however was conquered by the Holy Roman Empire in 962 and did not regain its independence until the 13th century. The last of the Premyslids was assassinated in 1306. The royal house of Luxembourg then entered Czech history when John married Princess Elisabeth Premysl. The result of this union was the Holy Roman Emperor Charles IV who sought to make Prague one of the great capitals of Europe.

Charles IV of Luxembourg (1346–1378), did much to establish Prague as an important capital and city: he commissioned the building of Charles Bridge, built a new district (the New Town) and also founded the first university in central Europe.

The cobbled streets of the city (such as Nový Svet above) are a pleasure to discover.

At the start of the 15th century, Jan Hus, the rector of Prague University, denounced the abuses and excesses then prevalent in the Church. He was excommunicated as an heretic in 1412, but today his teachings are still followed by the Hussites, a group of Czech Protestants.

In 1526, Ferdinand of Habsburg was made king. Later, under the Jesuits, Prague was to wholeheartedly embrace the Baroque movement. Over the centuries, however, the Habsburg domination was gradually eroded and at the beginning of the 19th century Bohemia witnessed a veritable 'national awakening'. The Republic of Czechoslovakia was proclaimed in 1918 and dissolved in 1939 by the Nazi occupation.

Today Prague is one of the most beautiful capitals in Europe.

In 1948, three years after the liberation of Prague by the Red Army, the Communist party swept to victory. During the 'Prague Spring' of 1968, Alexander Dubcek tried to offer the country 'socialism with a human face', but on August 21 of that year the tanks of the Warsaw Pact (excluding Romania) rolled into Czechoslovakia. Prague was to remain isolated from the rest of the world for the next twenty years. In 1989, the 'Velvet Revolution' brought Vaclav Havel to power as President of Czechoslovakia. Since then the country has split into two with Prague becoming the capital of the Czech Republic.

The 'Velvet Revolution' started with a demonstration and call for a general strike by students, artists and dissident intellectuals. In the face of public demand, the government was eventually forced to back down.

An art nouveau masterpiece. St Cyril and St Methodius give their blessing to St Vitus's Cathedral in this modern stained-glass window by Alfons Mucha.

The area around Prague Castle is full of many palaces, churches and monasteries, each one more impressive than the next.

The Belvedere.

Hradcany

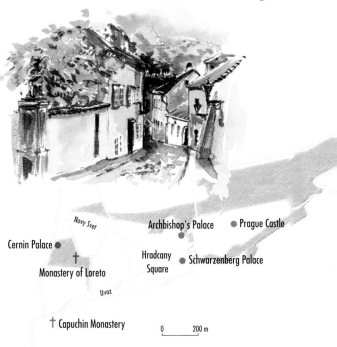

Novy Svet

Archbishop's Palace ● Prague Castle

Cernin Palace ●

Hradcany Square

● Schwarzenberg Palace

† Monastery of Loreto

Uvoz

† Capuchin Monastery

0   200 m

As night falls, the city and the Vltava are illuminated by the light from Prague Castle, dominating its surroundings as the symbol of Czech statehood.

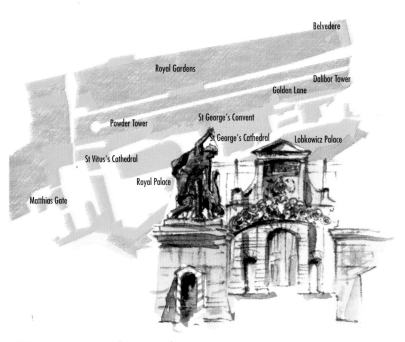

Belvedere

Royal Gardens

Dalibor Tower

Golden Lane

Powder Tower

St George's Convent

St George's Cathedral

Lobkowicz Palace

St Vitus's Cathedral

Royal Palace

Matthias Gate

Prague Castle

Prague Castle, now the official residence of the President of the Czech Republic, has almost always been at the heart of national government. Steeped in history, its walls are

The blue uniforms worn by the presidential guards on sentry duty in the main courtyard of the castle were commissioned by Václav Havel from the designer who worked on the films of the internationally famous Czech film director, Milos Forman.

filled with the memories of kings going back over a thousand years.

St Vitus's Cathedral and the two towers of St George's Basilica.

The statues of Fighting Giants standing at the entrance to the castle are copies of 18th-century sculptures by Platzer.

The changing of the guard, which takes place every hour in front of Prague Castle, is an extremely popular tourist attraction.

In Hradcanske namesti (**Hradcany Square**), two soldiers of the presidential guard stand at the main entrance to the castle while two statues of Fighting Giants flank the gate to the main courtyard, or court of honour, which dates from the 18th century. At the far end, the Matthias Gate leads to the second courtyard, overlooked by the President's office, where the old stables have been turned into a picture gallery.

The Matthias Gate links the first two courtyards of the castle. It was built in 1614 for the Emperor Matthias who succeeded Rudolph II of Habsburg.

The former prison in the menacing Dalibor tower is now open to the public.

The third courtyard is by far the largest, containing the castle churches, the Royal Palace and the Lobkowicz Palace. As you make your way towards the rear of the citadel, you pass the door of the old Renaissance palace of the Burgrave. The terrace

Stands selling all kinds of souvenirs and knick-knacks line the old steps (left) which lead from Prague Castle down to the underground station of Malostranka.

of the adjacent Cerna vez (Black Tower) offers an unobstructed view over the city. At the top of the old steps stands the **Dalibor Tower**, the infamous prison which was used

The Vltava is also known by its German name, the Moldau, due to the fact that German was the official language used by the Czech government until the 19th century.

until 1781. The tower is named after Dalibor of Kozojedy, the first prisoner to be incarcerated there. This young knight was condemned to death for having harboured fugitive serfs and held in an underground cell, into which his jailers had lowered him on the end of a rope. Whilst in solitary confinement, Dalibor learnt to play the violin and the inhabitants of Prague, touched by his melancholy playing, passed him food through an air shaft and thus kept him from starvation. An opera by the Czech composer Bedrich Smetana tells the story of Prague's most famous prisoner.

A short history of the castle

Between the time of its foundation by the Premysl princes and the creation of the Republic, Prague Castle witnessed the rise and fall of several dynasties. After ruling Bohemia for over 400 years, the Premyslids were succeeded by the Luxembourgs at the beginning of the 14th century. Charles IV, their most famous member, became King of Bohemia and Holy Roman Emperor. In the 15th century, George of Podebrady, the victor of the Hussite wars, was proclaimed King of Bohemia by the Estates-General. The only Protestant Czech king, he was succeeded by Vladislav Jagiello, son of the King of Poland. In the 16th century, the Habsburgs re-established a hereditary monarchy which lasted four hundred years.

The Golden Portal of St Vitus's Cathedral is topped by a Renaissance bell tower with a baroque cupola.

The southern entrance to St George's Basilica.

The Castle Churches

St Vitus's Cathedral, within the walls of Prague Castle, dates back to the 10th century, whilst the nearby St George's Basilica, with its two white towers, was

There is a chapel in the nave of St Vitus's Cathedral, near the organ and the new sacristy, where you can admire the vibrant colours of this modern stained-glass window that is attributed to Alfons Mucha, the Czech master of Art Nouveau.

once the privileged spectator of life in medieval Bohemia.

The pediment of St Vitus's Cathedral.

St Vitus's was built on the site of a Roman rotunda dating from the time of Wenceslas. When the church later became a cathedral in the 14th century, a chapel dedicated to Wenceslas was built on the exact site of the old Roman rotunda and still houses the saint's body.

In 1344, the bishopric of Prague was elevated to the rank of archbishopric. The construction of the beautiful Katedrala sv Vita (**St Vitus's Cathedral**) began as a result and was not completed until 1929! The future King Charles IV commissioned the services of the French Gothic master Matthieu d'Arras. He was succeeded on his death by his pupil Peter Parler who built the Gothic chancel, remarkable for the breathtaking columns

The Chapel of St Wenceslas was built on the site of the Roman Rotunda of St Vitus.

and star-covered vault. He was also responsible for the delicate blind arcades of the porch over the Golden Portal and the primary structure of one of the chapels dedicated to St Wenceslas, the Czech patron saint. On the door of this chapel is a bronze ring in the shape of a lion onto which Prince Wenceslas supposedly clung before dying. Inside, frescoes encrusted with some 1300 semi-precious stones depict scenes from the life of the saint. This chapel leads to the Treasure Chamber where the crown jewels, exhibited only on public holidays during leap years, are kept.

It was in 935 that Prince Wenceslas, a devout Christian, was assassinated on the orders of his brother Boleslav I during a religious service. He died while holding the ring on the door of the Rotunda of St Vitus.

The 16th-century royal mausoleum houses the remains of Ferdinand I, his wife and their son, Maximilian II.

The building of St Vitus's Cathedral was carried out over almost six centuries, held up by the Hussite wars (from the 15th to the 17th centuries).

A detail from the Golden Portal which is also adorned by a splendid 14th-century Venetian mosaic depicting a scene from The Last Judgement. The newly elected President of the Czech Republic addresses the people from a balcony opposite the Golden Portal.

The crypt of the Chapel of the Holy Cross.

St Vitus's Cathedral was also the place where the kings of Bohemia were crowned and buried and the remains of the country's greatest rulers and their wives can be found there. The crypt of the Chapel of the Holy Cross contains the tombs of the kings Charles IV (and his four wives), Wenceslas IV, George of Podebrady and Rudolph II. In the centre

The tomb of St John Nepomuk in the nave of the cathedral.

of the nave, the more recent royal mausoleum houses the tomb of Ferdinand I, the first Habsburg to rule Bohemia during the 16th century. St John Nepomuk, a famous national martyr, is also buried in the nave of the cathedral. Angels of Herculean strength bear his elaborate silver tomb which weighs almost two tonnes!

More than two tonnes of silver were used to make the ornate tomb of St John Nepomuk. He was thrown into the Vltava River on the orders of Wenceslas IV and was only made a saint in 1729 at the request of the Jesuits. Fischer von Erlach made his tomb in 1736. By making St John Nepomuk a saint, the Jesuits hoped to erase the memory of Jan Hus.

The flamboyantly coloured façade of St George's Basilica contrasts strikingly with the sober Roman style of the two towers and the inside of the building.

Statue to the right of the entrance.

The 12th-century St George's Basilica is one of the best preserved examples of Roman architecture remaining in Bohemia.

A carved wooden relief panel near the Chapel of St John the Baptist shows the state of Prague after the Battle of the White Mountain in 1620.

The Basilika sv Jiri (**St George's Basilica**) is a masterpiece of medieval Czech art, founded by Vratislav I in the 10th century. A convent was added shortly after. The basilica was rebuilt after a fire in the 12th century and baroque details were added during the 17th century. It contains the tombs of the Premysl rulers, Vratislav I, Boleslav II and Ludmilla.

St Ludmilla, the grandmother of Wenceslas, met a tragic end. She was strangled on the orders of her step-daughter Drahomira as she knelt to pray. Ludmilla died in 921 and shortly afterwards became Bohemia's first Christian martyr.

The Chapel of St Ludmilla is to the right of the chancel in St George's Basilica and contains the tomb of the first Premysl martyr.

The title of Abbess of St George's Convent conferred the privilege of crowning the queens of Bohemia, although the latter had no sovereign power.

Benedikt Ried was the architect of King Vladislav II Jagiello and was responsible for the 15th-century Vladislav Hall in the Royal Palace. Some of the work of the sculptor Ferdinand Brokoff, who worked on the Charles Bridge during the 18th century, is exhibited in the galleries of St George's Convent.

A detail from St George's Convent.

St George's Basilica is characterized by a wide range of artistic styles since all the greatest artists have left their mark on it over the centuries: Benedikt Ried was responsible for the portal whilst the statue of St John Nepomuk is by Ferdinand Maximilian Brokoff. The adjoining **St George's Convent** was once home to the first community of Benedictine nuns in

The inscription above the door of St George's Basilica.

Bohemia. The convent was founded in 973 by Prince Boleslav II whose sister, Mlada, was the first abbess. The community was broken up by Josef II in the 18th century and the building was used as a barracks until the middle of the 20th century. Since the 1970s, it has housed the magnificent collections of the National Gallery.

The museum of St George's Convent houses the Gothic and baroque work of Czech artists, including the painting of The Suicide of Lucretia by the German artist von Aachen that formed part of Rudolph II's own private collection. Other canvases such as those by Jan Kupecky, the Czech portrait painter of the baroque period, are also on display.

The Knights' Stairway added by Vladislav II Jagiello leads to the gigantic Vladislav Hall, both built by Benedikt Ried at the end of the 15th century.

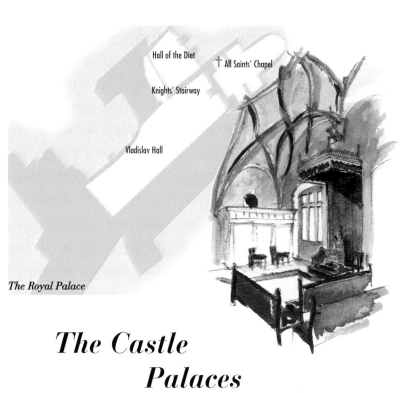

Hall of the Diet

† All Saints' Chapel

Knights' Stairway

Vladislav Hall

The Royal Palace

The Castle Palaces

The Royal Palace was once the residence of the various dynasties who ruled over the kingdom of Bohemia. Prague Castle also boasts a number of other large palaces,

The title of burgrave was given to the military commander in charge of a city or citadel during the time of the Holy Roman Empire (established in the 10th century and brought down by Napoleon). Deriving from the German word Burggraf, it means 'count of the fortress'.

including Lobkowicz Palace, now a museum, and the Burgrave's Palace.

The Gothic vaulting of Vladislav Hall.

The **Royal Palace** was built during the 12th century on the orders of Sobeslav I within the safety of the fortifications of Prague Castle. Until the great fire of 1541, each of the kings of Bohemia in turn added a personal touch to their

The great fire of 1541 not only devastated many of the Castle buildings but also large parts of Hradcany and Mala Strana.

home and a jumble of Roman and Gothic styles testifies to the architectural tastes of the various monarchs. On the first floor, Vladislav II Jaigello's extravagant hall is a

Frescoes adorn the ceiling of the banqueting hall in Lobkowicz Palace. The hall is the finest room in the palace and is sometimes used to host concerts.

unique achievement in flamboyant Gothic style. When required, this enormous hall could be transformed into a riding arena where wild jousting took place. The participants did not even have to dismount since the hall could be reached on horseback via the Knights' Stairway which was specially built to accommodate horses. Today, the President of the Czech Republic is appointed in the **Vladislav Hall** which is still known as the Chamber of Homage. The head of state takes an oath in the ancient hall in which the Diet (parliament) was held in the Middle Ages.

The Defenestration of Prague

On May 16, 1618, over a hundred Protestant nobles, weary of the policy of discrimination being directed against them, marched on the Royal Palace, the seat of the Estates-General of Bohemia. Under the leadership of Count Thurn, the men quarrelled with the Catholic representatives of Ferdinand II of Habsburg who had acceded to the throne of Bohemia a year earlier. Three men were pushed out of the window by the rebel Protestants but survived the 50-foot (16-metre) fall thanks to the presence of a dung heap. The 'defenestration of Prague' triggered the Thirty Years War between the Czech Protestants and the ruling Habsburgs, with the first victory going to the Catholics at the Battle of the White Mountain (1620).

All Saints' Chapel by Peter Parler was commissioned by Charles IV. The original construction was reworked in baroque style.

The sumptuous interior of Lobkowicz Palace, decorated with rich sgraffiti.

The beautiful **Lobkowicz Palace** near the Dalibor Tower is more modest in size. The original Renaissance sgraffiti on its façades and the baroque frescoes by Carlo Lurago in the banqueting room accurately reflect Bohemia's colourful history. Before heading for Golden Lane, a slight detour will take you to the old

Sgraffiti (from the Italian sgraffitto *meaning 'scratched') were very fashionable during the Renaissance period. Patterns were etched in a thin layer of white mortar that had been spread over, a background of a different colour.*

Burgrave's Palace which housed the Czech children's home during the Communist era.

The 'dolls' houses' of Golden Lane were built in the 16th century along the fortified walls in a quiet corner of Prague Castle.

A view of Powder Tower from the Royal Gardens.

Golden Lane and the Gardens

Those with a passion for mystery should head for Zlata ulicka (Golden Lane), whilst on the other side of the castle ramparts, a walk in the royal gardens will transport

Nowadays Golden Lane is no longer the place of intrigue that it once was. It has now been taken over by various shopkeepers selling books, glassware, cards, antiques and all kinds of souvenirs.

visitors back to the Renaissance and Baroque periods.

A shop window in Golden Lane.

Golden Lane owes its name to a rumour: during the 16th century, all sorts of odd experiments were said to have been carried out in these little multicoloured houses. The people of Prague were convinced that alchemists commissioned by the

Emperor Rudolph II spoke several languages including Czech. He embraced the spirit of the Renaissance, surrounding himself with artists and scientists.

emperor Rudolph II lived there and that they had succeeded in unlocking the secrets of the philosopher's stone, enabling them to change lead into gold. The inhabitants of

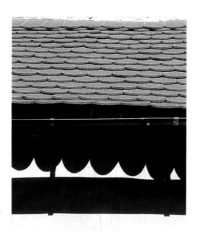

The writer Franz Kafka was, like so many others, enchanted by the mysterious atmosphere of Golden Lane. He lived there with his sister at no. 22 from 1916 to 1917.

Kafka, famous son of Prague

Franz Kafka hardly ever left the Czech capital where he was born in 1883 and whose air of mystery permeated his work. He wrote about the absurdity of existence, but only published one novel, *Metamorphosis*, during his lifetime. Kafka could not make a living out of writing and had to work in an insurance company. Like many authors who wrote in German, he frequented 'At the Golden Unicorn', a famous literary salon in the Old Town Square. In 1924 Kafka died of tuberculosis and his novels *The Castle* and *The Trial* were published shortly after his death. He is buried in the Jewish cemetery at Olsany, a small town on the outskirts of Prague.

Golden Lane were actually the whimsical emperor's guards rather than alchemists, living in houses that had been specially built to accommodate them. During the 17th century, jewellers moved there enabling the street to finally live up to its name, but it was then neglected for two hundred years and became a haunt of vagrants and criminals until the beginning of the 20th century when penniless artists moved in, rehabilitating the area and resurrecting the old tales about alchemy. The tiny houses that line the narrow lane were restored to their original state during the 1950s.

The houses of Golden Lane back onto the castle ramparts.

During the 16th century, the rich Jewish merchant Maisel amassed a huge fortune. When he died, however, no trace was found of this wealth. His family were suspected by the authorities of having hidden the money and were sent to prison. The case was not closed until 124 years later...

The rumours may have been wrong about Golden Lane but not about Rudolph II's intentions. Alchemists really were trying to change lead into gold in Prasna brana (**Powder Tower**) in the Old Town. The king, who regularly spent a fortune on works of art, had severe financial difficulties and was inclined to believe in miracles. Whether fact or fiction, it is said that Rudolph's coffers were suddenly filled with gold.

The Museum of Alchemey in Powder Tower.

According to Leo Perutz, a Prague-born writer and contemporary of Kafka, however, the upturn in the emperor's fortunes had more to do with an agreement made with a rich Jewish merchant, Mordechai Maisel, than with alchemy. Following the death of Rudolph II, Powder Tower was converted into a munitions store. It exploded in 1649 when the Swedish army was occupying the castle and in 1754 was converted into living quarters for the sacristans of St Vitus's Cathedral. The tower now houses a museum devoted to science and technology.

Rudolph II (1552-1612) was an eccentric. He chose Prague as his capital although his family, the Habsburgs, preferred Vienna. He was passionate about art and transformed Prague into the 'artistic treasure house of Europe'.

Prague Castle seen from the Royal Gardens.

Rudolph II took special care of a lion that he owned because it had been predicted that the animal's death would foreshadow his own.

The beautiful Renaissance Belvedere shown here behind the Singing Fountain was the summer palace of the Bohemian kings.

Rudolph II had an impressive collection of exotic wild beasts and had a private zoo built to house them. The emperor had a particular passion for lions which were fed on the finest meat from the district which later became known as Josefov (the Jewish Quarter). The lion house has now been converted into a restaurant whilst the old zoo is surrounded by beautiful gardens and colourful flower beds.

Two baroque lions inspiring little fear guard the entrance to the tranquil Royal Gardens.

As you approach Franceso Terzio's Singing Fountain (cast by Tomas Jaros), you can hear the gentle murmur of the water trickling into the bronze basin.

The Dance *by Alice Pittaluga.*

These pleasant gardens are the ideal setting for a long walk, especially since you are no longer likely to meet one of Rudolph II's lions!

Modern paintings by 20th-century Czech painters are exhibited in the former stables at the other end of the gardens to the Belvedere.

The garden has been redesigned in the style of the 17th and 18th centuries and behind its dense groves, the façade of the **Real Tennis Court** is decorated entirely with typical Renaissance sgraffiti. The **Belvedere**, or Summer Palace, standing opposite the classical garden that contains the Singing Fountain, is home to a magnificent art collection.

The Belvedere was built from the plans of the architect Paolo della Stella in the 16th century. The building has a magnificent copper roof in the shape of a ship's hull and is considered to be the most beautiful Renaissance building in this part of Europe.

The rococo façade of Archbishop's Palace was designed in the 18th century by Van Josef Wirch.

Strahov Monastery at the foot of Petrin hill.

Palaces and Monasteries in Hradcany

In the area around Prague Castle, old houses rub shoulders with baroque palaces, churches and monasteries. The awestruck visitor can happily spend many hours

The area immediately surrounding Prague Castle was reserved for the city's notables, whilst the Novy Svet district (which literally means New World), situated on the outskirts of Hradcany, was inhabited by those who worked at the Castle.

wandering around this amazing labyrinth of architectural marvels.

The castle and palaces in Hradcany Square.

Hradcanske namesti (**Hradcany Square**) is noted for the superb trompe l'oeil sgraffiti used to decorate the Schwarzenberg Palace. This Renaissance palace is now a museum of military history where the visitor can learn about the

On the edge of the castle complex, the Archbishop's Palace is a symbol of the close links between religious and political power introduced by the Catholic rulers, the Habsburgs.

strategies adopted by the Hussite generals in the 15th century. Close by, the **Sternberg Palace** houses the painting collections of the National Gallery. At the end of the 18th cen-

Count Cernin, the Ambassador to Venice, was determined to own the most luxurious residence around Prague Castle. He was, however, destined never to live there.

The Sternberg Palace Collection

The enormous Sternberg Palace collection extends over three floors. The works of artists from the last two centuries, such as Rodin, Rousseau and Picasso, is on the ground floor. On the first floor, which is dedicated to older Italian and Flemish work, visitors can admire *Haymaking* by Pieter Bruegel the Elder. On the second floor, the strange square halo of El Greco's *Head of Christ* lights up the gallery and Dürer's famous *Feast of the Rosary* hangs in an adjoining room. A little further on, Cranach the Elder's *Adam and Eve* casually flaunt their nudity in a way which never fails to surprise enthusiasts of Renaissance painting.

tury, Count Sternberg founded the Society of Patriotic Friends of the Arts in Bohemia. He persuaded art lovers to entrust him with their most beautiful pieces which are now exhibited in his palace. In Loretanske Square, the Venetian-style building, constructed for Count Cernin by Francesco Caratti during the 17th century, has thirty Corinthian columns along the 500 feet (150 metres) of its façade. The Cernin family, however, could not afford its upkeep and in the 19th century the palace was bought by the government and became the Ministry of Foreign Affairs.

The high altar of the Santa Casa. Catherine of Lobkowicz commissioned this building, believed to be a copy of the house of the Virgin Mary, in 1626.

In 1694, the Danish clockmaker Peter Naumann designed the mechanism that is used to ring the bells of the the Loreto.

The treasures of the the Loreto contain an ornate monstrance (the receptacle used for holding the conse-crated bread), studded with over 6000 diamonds. This price-less ritual object from Vienna is made of gilded silver and weighs more than 25 pounds.

The bell tower of the baroque monastery.

Opposite the Cernin Palace, the baroque monastery of Loreto and the contrastingly austere Capuchin monastery are joined by a covered passageway. The Monastery of Loreto (the **Loreto**) was built in the 17th century and has always been a major centre for pilgrims. The tower, with its 27 bells, soars above the cloisters which contain the Santa Casa.

The façade of the Monastery of Loreto was designed by the Deintzenhofers. The sculptures are the work of Kohl and Quittainer, 18th-century Czech artists.

The baroque sanctuary of the Loreto.

Legend has it that the Santa Casa is the house in Nazareth in which the Virgin was visited by the archangel Gabriel. In the 13th century this house was then miraculously transported to the Italian village of Loreto. The replica built in Prague dates from the 17th century.

The Church of the Nativity in the Loreto is decorated with baroque frescoes and contains many religious relics. Next to the Loreto, the rather sober 17th-century **Capuchin Monastery** (left) contrasts starkly with the other buildings in an area entirely given over to the baroque. It is devoid of any superfluous ornamentation that would disturb the peace and tranquillity which reign within its walls.

The Santa Casa holds pride of place in the very centre of the cloisters of the Loreto.

Emperor Rudolph II, on the other hand, was extremely troubled by a very strange occurrence. He greatly admired a wonderful statue of the Virgin and Child in the Church of Our Lady Queen of Angels in the Capuchin Monastery and, with the agreement of the monks, took it to his private chapel so that he could contemplate it without having to leave the castle. The statue miraculously returned to its original home three times! The emperor finally gave in to the statue's wishes and placated the Virgin by giving her a golden crown and splendid robe.

On Christmas Eve, the people of Prague gather in the Church of Our Lady Queen of Angels to see the charming baroque nativity scene with life-size figures dressed in period costume.

The walls of the Philosophical Hall are covered with old books.

The bell towers of Strahov rise high above the baroque monastery buildings which contain an organ that Mozart is said to have played.
The Theological Hall houses some wonderful 17th-century globes.

The Strahovsky klaster (**Strahov Monastery**) stands at the foot of Petrin hill. Founded in 1140 by an austere religious order known as the Premonstratensians, the monastery's riches were largely of an intellectual nature. It is famous for its abbey and collection of ancient books. The library is over eight hundred years old and is divided into two rooms, one dedicated to theology, the other to philosophy.

A detail from the ceiling fresco in the Theological Hall of Strahov Monastery. The main theme of this work is the exaltation of knowledge.

Tomasska Street, in the shadow of St Vitus's Cathedral and Prague Castle, is typical of Mala Strana (the Little Quarter).

Below the castle, the quaint old quarter of Mala Strana has defended its palaces and streets against the invasion of modern architecture.

A house sign in Nerudova Street.

Mala Strana

● Wallenstein Palace

† St Thomas's

Nerudova Street

Little Quarter Square

St Nicholas's †

Charles Bridge

Our Lady Victorious †

Maltese Square † Our Lady beneath the Chain

Petrin Park

Kampa

"Eiffel Tower" ●

Mirror Maze ●

Petrin funicular ●

● Hunger Wall

0   200 m

Enjoy a stroll around Mala Strana and enjoy the charms of the baroque architecture which bears testimony to the city's prosperity under the Habsburgs.

The dome of the Church of St Nicholas in Mala Strana.

Visitors are always surprised by the number of palaces on the left bank of the Vltava. The palaces of Ledebour-Trauttmansdorff, Auersperk, Palffy, Kolowrat-Cernin and Fürstenberg have two things in common: their baroque style and their location in **Valdstejnska Street**. The enormous Valdstejnsky palac (**Wallenstein Palace**) was

Wallenstein inherited a considerable fortune from his two rich wives. Having converted to Catholicism, this opportunist general made himself indispensable to an empire ravaged by the Thirty Years War, filling his coffers still further by swindling Czech Protestants.

built in the 17th century with the fortune that its owner tricked out of the Protestants.

The fountain of Venus in the courtyard of General Wallenstein's sumptuous palace.

General Wallenstein had an army of some twenty thousand men and owned quarter of Bohemia. This made him too powerful for the liking of Ferdinand II who had him assassinated as a result. In addition to its luxurious interior, the

Above: a statue found in Little Quarter Square.
Left: this bronze statue of Eros, a copy of a work by Adriaen de Vries, stands in the baroque gardens of Wallenstein Palace.

palace has a wonderful garden with a mytho-logical theme. The beautiful grottoes, decorated fountains, statues and groves are all true masterpieces of baroque art.

The sumptuous Ledebour Palace pictured here is also famous for its 18th-century gardens which are stepped and terraced in the style associated with the Italian Renaissance.

The signs of Mala Strana

Coloured signs adorn the façades of the old houses all along Nerudova Street. These signs were used to distinguish the houses before numbering was introduced in 1770. The house 'At the Three Violins' was owned by makers of stringed instruments for several generations, but now provides visitors with instruments of a different nature, namely knives and forks. Now 12 Nerudova Street, it caters more for gastronomes than for musicians. Like many of the houses in this street, made famous by the poet and journalist Jan Neruda, it has been converted into a restaurant which is highly rated by gourmets.

Mala Strana was ravaged by both the Hussite wars of the 15th century and the great fire of 1541. As a result, Renaissance buildings were erected on the ruins of the Middle Ages. In 1620, however, the Austrians invaded the Bohemian capital and, under Jesuit influence, imposed their own Catholic culture and style of architecture. During the 17th and 18th centuries, baroque palaces gradually replaced Renaissance buildings although some of the latter survived, as seen in Malostranske namesti (**Little Quarter Square**) where the two styles mingle.

The baroque nave of the Church of St Thomas.

Dolls, puppets and wooden toys are just some of the typical specialities made by the craftsmen of Prague.

Uvoz Street is the continuation of Nerudova Street and like the latter contains many baroque façades (pictured right).

The baroque Kostel sv Tomase (the **Church of St Thomas**) is situated directly behind the gardens of Wallenstein Palace. During the 18th century, Kilian Ignac Dientzenhofer renovated this 13th century church and, retaining the Gothic spire, made the building his own masterpiece. Just beside the church, the city's oldest bar serves a special dark beer in its vaulted cellar. Going towards Little Quarter Square you

Nerudova Street leads from Prague Castle to Little Quarter Square.

rejoin Nerudova Street, named after the Prague-born poet and journalist Jan Neruda. This great 19th-century storyteller described the district in *Stories from Mala Strana*. In the 18th century, Mozart and his friend Casanova attended balls held at the Bretfeld Palace at 33 Nerudova Street. Some of the houses have picturesque and colourful names: number 34 is 'At the Golden Horseshoe' and number 43 'At the Green Lobster'. Beer must once have been sold at number 45 since the sign of the 'Black Lion' shows a lion holding a tankard between its paws.

Nerudova Street is rich in legend and local colour. Nowadays, it boasts a number of very popular wine bars and pubs where the locals often meet in the evening for a drink.

The bell towers of the Church of St Nicholas rise above Little Quarter Square and serve as a useful landmark in the city of a hundred towers.

The frescoes adorning the nave of the Church of St Nicholas.

Chram sv Mikulase (the **Church of St Nicholas**) was inherited by the Jesuits in the 17th century after the Protestant defeat at the Battle of the White Mountain. It is a baroque masterpiece that was created between 1703 and 1735 by three generations of the Dientzenhofer family. The statues decorating the facade are the work of John Frederik Kohl while Franz Xaver Palko painted the frescoes in the cupola which is 246 feet (75 metres) high!

The pulpit (from 1765) is the epitome of High Baroque and is the masterpiece of Richard and Peter Prachner.

In front of the Church of St Nicholas, the tall plague column commemorates the end of the epidemic that struck in 1715.

Renaissance-style houses around the Church of St Nicholas.

It took almost fifty years to build the Church of St Nicholas, spanning three generations of architect from the same family. Christoph Dientzenhofer was followed by his son Kilian Ignac with the work being completed by the latter's son-in-law, Anselmo Lurago.

No praise is too great when describing the Church of St Nicholas: the fresco depicting scenes from the life of the saint covers over 16,000 square feet (1500 square metres) and took 18th-century artist Jan Lukas Kraker nearly ten years to complete. The sculptures, including a copper statue of St Nicholas, are by Platzer the Elder. It is generally considered to be the world's finest example of a baroque church.

The statue of St John the Baptist in the centre of Maltese Square.

Maltezske namesti (**Maltese Square**) is situated near Karmelitska Street and testifies to the wealth of the Knights of Malta. In the 12th century, Vladislav II met members of the order during campaigns in the Holy Land. He decided to build a fortified church in their honour and the knights erected a commander's residence at the entrance to Judith Bridge (no longer standing, but near the site of the current Charles Bridge). This bridge was said to have been closed off with a golden chain, reflected in the name given to the church, Our Lady beneath the Chain.

In 1796, the German composer Ludwig van Beethoven, then aged 26, lived in a pretty house in Lazenska Street called 'At the Golden Unicorn'. This house faces the Church of Our Lady beneath the Chain.

The windows of the houses divulge few secrets, even when they are open.

As a place of pilgrimage, the Church of Our Lady Victorious (pictured right) is famous throughout the Christian world. Inside, the wax statue of the Holy Infant of Prague. (known by its Italian name il Bambino di Praga) is Spanish in origin and stands on a richly decorated alter.

In 1620, the Carmelites were given the Protestant Church of the Holy Trinity in return for their collaboration with the Catholic forces during the Battle of the White Mountain. They renamed it the Church of Our Lady Victorious. In 1628, it became a place of pilgrimage renowned throughout the Christian world due to a wax statue of the Infant Jesus that is said to have been responsible for many miracles.

Mostecka (or Bridge) Street has linked Little Quarter Square with Charles Bridge for over 750 years. Here you can see the tower of Mala Strana Bridge.

A carving from the romantic Na Kampe Squares.

In the old garden of the Knights of Malta in Grand Priory Square you can still see the graffiti depicting John Lennon which has graced the wall since his death. It acted as a rallying point for the young people of Prague during the period when the music of the ex-Beatles singer was banned.

Heading back down towards the Vltava, you will find the delightful island of Kampa which was given to the Knights of Malta by Vladislav II and subsequently became the haunt of artists inspired by its charm. The island is separated from Mala Strana by a branch of the Vltava known as the Certovka which literally means 'Devil's Stream'. There used to be a pottery market around **Na Kampe Square** but now a park made

Grand Priory Mill was is use from the 16th century until 1936.

up of the combined gardens of several old palaces offers magnificent views over the Stare mesto (Old Town). Further along, the restored water wheel of Grand Priory Mill turns aimlessly on the calm water of the Certovka. The mill, which once ground the corn of the Knights of Malta, now lies idle. At the other end of Kampa Island, below Charles Bridge, a group of houses, known as 'the Venice of Prague', are built directly on the waters edge. The main difference with Venice being that small boats rather than gondolas ply the calm waters of this branch of the river.

The Devil's Stream is not as satanic as it sounds. This branch of the Vltava was, in fact, named in the 19th century after a woman of 'strong character' who lived nearby in a house on Maltese Square.

From the Petrin Gardens you can enjoy a magnificent view over Prague.

Half way up Petrin hill, the funicular stops at the famous Nebozizek restaurant. Here you can enjoy breathtaking views over Prague Castle and the city whilst dining in style. Afterwards, why not enjoy a gentle stroll in the Petrin Gardens?

Petrin Park on the slopes of Petrin Hill was created from ancient gardens and vineyards established here during the 12th century. As you travel up the hill in the funicular there is a superb view over the city. At the top, through an arch in Hunger Wall, you will find the Observation Tower, a 200-foot (60-metre) copy of the Eiffel tower, built for the Jubilee Exhibition in 1891. The Mirror Maze, also built for the 1891 Exhibition and moved to Petrin shortly afterwards, stands near the baroque Church of St Lawrence and will interest young and old alike. Lower down, the Church of St

Mozart's harpsichord at the Villa Bertramka.

Michael of Petrin was rebuilt in 1929. The wooden chapel was a gift from the inhabitants of a village in the Carpathians, a region annexed by the Republic of Czechoslovakia after World War I. A short excursion to the Villa Bertramka on the outskirts of Prague, south of Petrin, is a must for Mozart lovers. The famous composer stayed

It is said that Mozart composed the overture to his opera Don Giovanni *while staying at the Villa Bertramka with his wife as guests of the composer Dusek in 1787. The house is now a museum dedicated to his creative genius.*

there towards the end of his life and the building now contains a museum dedicated to him.

Statues of Saints Norbert, Wenceslas and Sigismund stand just beside the cross marking the place where St John Nepomuk was thrown into the Vltava.

Built to link the two settlements on either side of the Vltava, Charles Bridge spans the river, uniting the impressive cityscapes.

The lights of Charles Bridge.

Charles Bridge

Certovka

Vlatva

Little Quarter Bridge Tower ● ● St Vitus

● St John Nepomuk

● Sts Norbert, Wenceslas and Sigismund
● Crucifix

Judith Bridge Tower ●

● St Luitgard

St Ludmilla ●

Pietà ●

● Old Town Bridge Tower

Charles Bridge and the towers of the Old Town.

The entrance to Karluv most (**Charles Bridge**) from Mala Strana is very imposing, with the two towers of Judith Bridge and Little Quarter Bridge framing the entrance to Prague's most famous piece of architecture. This Gothic bridge was built by Peter Parler during the 14th century after being commissioned by Charles IV. The latter went as far as to consult his astrologers to find out the most favourable time to lay the first stone.

All along the bridge, from Little Quarter Bridge Tower to Old Town Bridge Tower, craftworkers and artists sell their work.

From Charles Bridge you can enjoy this view of the castle silhouetted against the sky.

St Vitus, spared by the lions, in front of Little Quarter Bridge Tower.

The statues of St Vitus and St Luitgard are two of the most impressive sculptures, whilst tradition has it that it is lucky to touch the statue of St John Nepomuk. A figure of Christ dating from the 18th century now stands on the site of what was once the bridge's only decoration, a wooden crucifix. A Jew accused of blasphemy was forced to pay for the Hebrew inscription around the figure of Christ which reads 'holy, holy, holy God'.

At the end of the Thirty Years War, a truce was signed with the Swedish army in the middle of Charles Bridge. This armistice saved the Old Town from being destroyed, though a number of works of art from the collection of Rudolph II were plundered and carried off to Sweden.

Prague by night: Charles Bridge.

At the end of the bridge is Old Town Bridge Tower, built by the Gothic master Peter Parler. The tower, once used as a prison, carries the statues of Charles IV, Wenceslas IV and the guardian saints of the bridge, Saints Wenceslas, Adalbert and Sigismund. In 1621, during the peak of conflicts between Catholics and Hussites, the heads of ten Protestant nobles were displayed there as a sign of Habsburg domination.

This Gothic detail shows the coat of arms of the Old Town on the tower marking the entrance to the district. The stone carvings are the work of Peter Parler.

The astronomical clock with its animated figures at the Old Town Hall is the most fascinating relic of the Middle Ages in Prague.

The path of the old Coronation Procession taken by the princes of Bohemia crosses Stare Mesto, the medieval quarter of Prague.

The towers of Our Lady before Tyn.

Stare Mesto

St Nicholas †
● Golz-Kinsky Palace
† Our Lady before Tyn
Old Town Hall ●
Celetna
Clementinum ●
● "At the Two Golden Bears"   "At the Black Madonna"
● Carolinum
Karlova
● Smetana Museum
Husova
Havelka
Naprstkova
Na Prikope
Smetanovo Nabrezi
Karoliny svetle
Skorepka
Perlova
Na Perstyne
0   200 m
Narodni

Behind the arcades of these houses of Roman origin lie the Franz Kafka gallery, the U Bindru restaurant and a tourist information office.

The coat of arms of the Old Town: a detail from the façade of the Old Town Hall.

Old Town Square

Staromestske namesti (Old Town Square) is an amazing place. At the Town Hall, the astronomical clock measures the passage of time in this lively square situated at the

Old Town Square is surrounded on all sides by historical monuments. The ancient Royal Route to the west leads away to Charles Bridge. The 14th-century university, or Carolinum, lies to the south and Powder Tower and Municipal House to the east.

very heart of the city, surrounded by medieval monuments.

The towers of Our Lady before Tyn soar above Old Town Square.

The towers and statues of the Church of St Nicholas rise high above Old Town Square. The church was built between 1732 and 1735 by Kilian Ignac Dientzenhofer, the master of baroque style. It has been a Hussite church since 1920.

Jan Hus, the symbol of Czech freedom of thought, occupies a place of honour in Old Town Square. The statue, sculpted by Ladislav Saloun to mark the 500th anniversary of the reformer's execution, commemorates the persecution of the Hussites and the enforced exile of the Protestants. The statue, erected in 1915, features the figure of a young mother holding her child, symbolizing the rebirth of the nation.

Jan Hus, precursor of the Reformation, was condemned for heresy by the Council of Constance and burnt at the stake in 1415.

The coat of arms of Golz-Kinsky Palace, next to Our Lady before Tyn.

Municipal House is a beautiful art nouveau building that was designed by the architect Polívka in 1868. It was originally built for the Prague city insurance company on the site of the Royal Court Palace.

On the other side of the square stands the 18th-century rococo Golz-Kinsky Palace. Designed by Kilian Ignac Dientzenhofer, this building is decorated with red stucco work, porches supported by Corinthian columns, balconies and numerous sculptures. The palace bears the name of the imperial diplomat, Stepan Kinsky, who bought it from the Golz family. It is the birthplace of Countess Kinsky, the future

A view of Stare Mesto from the tower of the Old Town Hall.

Bertha von Suttner, who was awarded the Nobel Peace Prize in 1905 for her work towards disarmament. In 1948, the victory of the Communist party was proclaimed from the palace balconies. Some of the collections of the National Gallery are now on display here. To the right of Golz-Kinsky Palace, at the entrance to the house 'At the Stone Bell', a plaque states that Franz Kafka lived in this restored Gothic house for a time. The tower of the Old Town Hall is 230 feet (70 metres) high and gives a view over the square and, on a clear day, part of Bohemia too.

Old Town Square is a popular haunt with tourists. Its timeless charm attracts both young and old who come to eat and drink in the pavement cafés and restaurants in summer.

The face of the astronomical clock is decorated with the signs of the zodiac.

Staromestska radnice (the **Old Town Hall**) was built in the 14th century and extended over time to encroach upon the adjoining houses. This symbol of the Bohemian capital was carefully restored following the damage caused by the Nazis during the Prague Uprising in 1945. At the bottom of the tower, a wonderful clock captivates passers-by. The **astronomical clock**, dating from the end of the 15th

Above: one of the coats of arms on the ceiling of the Old Town Hall. This building also has a number of Protestant Czech treasures, including the painting of Brozik depicting Jan Hus before the Council of Constance.

The town hall astronomical clock traces the orbits of the Sun and Moon around the Earth and their movement through the signs of the zodiac.

An astronomical mechanism

This clock has been measuring the passage of time in Prague for more than 500 years. It was built by Hanus, a master clockmaker who, according to the legend, was blinded to prevent him from reproducing his masterpiece elsewhere. The mechanism was perfected by Jan Taborsky in the 16th century but the ingenious principle by which it works has remained unchanged despite numerous repairs. The main function of the Town Hall clock is to calculate the paths of the heavenly bodies rather than show the right time. The outer circle, marked with 24 Arabic numerals, displays time as it used to be calculated in Bohemia during the Middle Ages. The three-coloured inner disc, marked with 24 Roman numbers, marks standard time.

century, is the relic of an era when people believed that the Earth was at the centre of the universe. Every hour, just before the clock strikes, spectators gather to watch the procession of figurines, triggered by the clock's mechanism. These figures include Death who turns over his hourglass and sounds the death knell, a Turk who shakes his head, Vanity looking at himself in a mirror, Greed and the 12 Apostles who appear behind St Peter. At the end of this enchanting spectacle, a cockerel flaps its wings and crows in time to the striking clock and the Apostles file back inside.

The Gothic style of Our Lady before Tyn, its spires topped with slender turrets, blends perfectly into the architectural composition of Stare mesto.

Our Lady before Tyn looks like something out of a fairy tale.

Another spectacular sight in the Old Town Square is the 14th-century Tynsky chram (**Our Lady before Tyn**). This was once the main Hussite Church in Prague and its façade was adorned with a golden chalice given by the Hussite king, George of Podebrady. After the Battle of the White Mountain in 1620, the victorious Catholics melt-

During the 15th century, the fine Gothic church of Our Lady before Tyn rivalled St Vitus's Cathedral in importance and was, until 1620, the main Hussite church in Prague. The only archbishop in its history was Jan Rokycana.

ed down the gold to make the aureole of the Virgin which can now be seen between the towers.

The steps to the Gothic pulpit of Our Lady before Tyn.

Horse-drawn carriages are the only form of transport that is allowed to cross the Old Town Square.

The 16th century astronomer Tycho Brahe proved that comets were not atmospheric phenomena.

From the 17th century onwards, the Jesuits were zealous in their efforts to efface the Protestant Gothic elements of the church in favour of the Baroque. However, a Passion of Christ that dates from 1390, a Madonna, the Gothic pulpit and baptismal fonts from 1414 (the oldest in the city) survived the changes. To the right of the altar is the tomb of the Danish astronomer to Rudolph II, Tycho Brahe.

The Golden Virgin takes pride of place between the two towers of Our Lady before Tyn, a reminder that this old Hussite Church fell into the hands of the Catholics.

Powder Gate at the end of Celetna Street stands on the site of one of the thirteen gates which allowed access to the fortified medieval city.

The airy interior of the Church of the Holy Saviour in the Clementinum.

The Royal Route

The old Kralovska cesta (Royal Route), including the section from Charles Bridge to Powder Gate, has been witness to the city's most elegant royal processions,

Begun in 1475 as a coronation gift from the city to King Vladislav II, Powder Gate was not completed until the 19th century. Its name derives from the fact that during the 17th century the tower was used to store gunpowder and munitions.

following what now forms Celetna Street and Karlova Street.

'At the Golden Snake', the oldest cafe in Prague at 18 Karlova Street, was opened in 1714 by an Armenian who used it to distribute political pamphlets.

The façade of U Rott's, an old ironmonger's shop, decorated by Mikulas Ales.

Behind the Old Town Hall, in the little square called Male namesti, stands the ornate façade of U Rott's ironmonger's shop. **Celetna Street**, on the way to Powder Gate is now reserved for pedestrians and horse-drawn carriages and is a part of the Royal Route that is very busy. The cubist house 'At the Black Madonna' at 34

'At the Black Madonna' (opposite) is a cubist house that is now a café. This particular style of architecture marks the end of Austro-Hungarian cultural domination in Prague and coincided with a period of national awakening.

Celetna Street, built by Joseph Gokar in 1912, is one of the architectural curiosities of the city.

The fruit market in Havelska Street is one of the most picturesque in Prague.

The house 'At the Two Golden Bears' near the Old Town Square has a magnificent Renaissance doorway.

The German composer Ludwig van Beethoven performed several of his works in the private theatre at Clam-Gallas Palace.

The **Carolinum** stands at the crossroads of Zelezna Street and Ovocny Street. This eminent university, founded in the 14th century by Charles IV, was rebuilt in Gothic style in 1945. It is the oldest educational institution in central Europe but is no longer used as a place of learning. A detour to Clam-Gallas Palace before rejoining Karlova Street will enable you to admire Matyas Braun's four enormous statues of Hercules.

Overlooked by bell towers, Karlova Street, which leads from the Old Town Square to Charles Bridge, is full of shops, hotels, restaurants, theatres and cinemas.

The Clementinum is the largest complex of buildings in Prague after the castle. It was a Jesuit college until 1773 and now houses the National Library.

Old Town Bridge Tower and the dome of the Church of St Francis.

Going back down Karlova Street, you will come across Princess Libuse and her falcons at number 24. A little further on is the enormous Clementinum with its many churches. As you head towards the Vltava you will see Old Town Bridge Tower framed between Knights of the Cross Square, with its statue of Charles IV, on the

This statue of Charles IV was erected in 1848 in order to mark the 500th anniversary of the Carolinum.

A museum about the life of the Czech composer Bedrich Smetana was opened in an old water tower in 1936.

right and the Smetana museum, noted for its rich neo-Renaissance façade, on the left.

The east façade of the Old-New Synagogue. This 13th-century Gothic sanctuary is the oldest synagogue in Europe.

Josefov, the name given to the old ghetto in Prague after King Joseph II, is a place where history has become entangled with myth.

A detail from the Klausen Synagogue.

Josefov

St Agnes's Convent

Rudolfinum

Jewish Cemetery ✡   ✡ Old-New Synagogue

✡ Klausen Synagogue

Jan Palach Square   ✡   ● Town Hall

Pinkas Synagogue

0   200 m

Old Quarter Square

Parizka Street crosses Josefov, linking the Old Town Square and the Vltava.

At the end of the 16th century, the rich merchant Mordechai Maisel became mayor of Josefov and gave money to fund the building of the town hall (opposite).

The cubist houses built in Josefov at the beginning of the 20th century are not to be missed.

All that really remains of the old Jewish ghetto in Prague are the synagogues and the town hall which was built at the end of the 16th century. The squalid and dilapidated old houses were pulled down at the end of the 19th century, shortly after Josefov became part of the city of Prague. The clock on **Josefov Town Hall** appears to go backwards: it turns anticlockwise, just as Hebrew script runs from right to left.

According to legend, the streets of Josefov sometimes witness the appearance of a mythical creature, the Golem, which comes back to haunt the area every 33 years.

Many thousands of people lie buried under the 12,000 or so tombstones crammed together in the Old Jewish Cemetery.

The Old-New Synagogue is the oldest Jewish sanctuary in Europe.

Close by, the Golem is re-puted to sleep in the attic of the **Old-New Synagogue** which dates from the 13th century. Rabbi Löw, the creator of this legendary creature, is buried in Stary zidovsky hrbitov (the **Old Jewish cemetery**). His tomb, covered with small stones and papers inscribed with prayers, is the most famous in the cemetery. Mordechai Maisel, a wealthy merchant and mayor of Josefov, is also buried there.

In the Old-New Synagogue, two Renaissance-style pillars flank the Ark where the precious Torah is kept. Next to them stands the chair of Rabbi Löw which has been used by all the chief rabbis of Prague since the 16th century.

The oldest tomb in the Old Jewish Cemetry belongs to Rabbi Avigdor Kara (1439). The most recent, that of Moses Beck, dates from 1787.

The façade of Pinkas Synagogue.

The Golem is a creature from Jewish folklore. In the 16th century, Rabbi Löw is supposed to have used a magic stone tablet to endow his clay figure with life.

Prominent members of the Jewish community in Prague are commemorated in the Klausen Synagogue where many ritual objects have been kept since the end of the Nazi occupation. Himmler wanted to preserve the Jewish ghetto as an 'exotic museum of an extinct race'.

Near the Old Jewish Cemetery, the baroque **Klausen Synagogue** houses an exhibition dealing with the history and traditions of Jews living in central Europe since the Middle Ages. Drawings of children imprisoned in the concentration camp in Terezin Castle are also on display. Close by, **Pinkas Synagogue** memorial bears the names of some 77,300

The neo-Renaissance façade of the Rudolfinum is adorned with statues of artists.

Jews who were sent from Czechoslovakia to the Nazi death camps. As you make your way towards the Vltava, you will come to the home of the Czech Philharmonic Orchestra, the **Rudolfinum**. This building was erected in honour of Rudolph II and during the Spring Festival, large concerts are held there in the superb Dvorak Hall.

At the north end of Josefov, St Agnes's Convent ranks as one of the city's most beautiful Gothic buildings. It was founded in 1234 by the sister of Wenceslas I and abandoned at the end of the 18th century. It was restored during the 1960s and finally converted into a museum used by the National Gallery to display a collection of 19th century Czech paintings.

Outside the National Museum, the statue of St Wenceslas on horseback watches over the busiest shopping square in the heart of Nove Mesto.

Nove Mesto, or the New Town, celebrated its 650th anniversary in 1998. It boasts a wide range of styles from medieval to modern.

A baroque fairy tale frog prince.

Nove Mesto

National Theatre

Jungmannova

Wenceslas Square

U Fleku bar

New Town Hall

National Museum

Zitna

St Cyril and St Methodius

Resslova

Charles Square

Jecna

Na Morani

Jesuit College

Faust House

Dvorak Museum

Na Slovanech Monastery

Trojicka

Botanical Gardens

Ke Karlovu

0   200 m

The art nouveau façade of the Grand Hotel Evropa. The original decor of this building has been preserved throughout, except in the bedrooms.

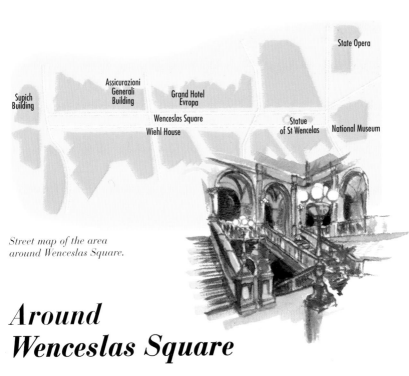

Street map of the area
around Wenceslas Square.

Around
Wenceslas Square

Vaclavske namesti
(Wenceslas Square) in
the centre of Nove
Mesto was once a
horse market and is
still the commercial
heart of the city. From
astride his horse, St

*The dimensions of
Wenceslas Square
are impressive: 820
yards (750 metres)
long and 66 yards
(60 metres) wide.
In front of the art
nouveau façades
and rich window
displays of this
square, the Czech
people have often
dreamed of win-
ning their freedom.*

Wenceslas overlooks the square which
has witnessed many terrible events.

The magnificent Grand Hotel Evropa was built at the beginning of the 20th century.

Art Nouveau first appeared in the city to mark the jubilee in 1891. A large number of buildings were built in this style, particularly in the areas of Josefov and Nove Mesto. The fine elegant lines of art nouveau architecture helped to restore these run-down areas.

The late 19th-century **Wiehl House** which stands opposite the Mustek underground station on Wenceslas square is named after its architect, but the finest art nouveau building in Prague is without doubt the **Grand Hotel Evropa**. Its charming early 20th-century architecture is intact; the façade is decorated with elaborate balconies and gilded nymphs and the restaurant is resplendent with mosaics, chandeliers and mirrors.

The entire art nouveau façade of Wiehl House is elaborately painted, some of it by Mikulas Ales. The building itself is neo-Renaissance in style.

At night, the clock on the Supich Building lights up Wenceslas Square.

The pedestrianized Na Prikope Street, at the foot of the Supich Building, is one of the busiest in the city.

Opposite: clean geometric lines of the art nouveau façade of the Supich Building.

The **Supich Building** at 38 Wenceslas Square is the old headquarters of a Moravian bank. The building is one of Mataj Blecha's grandest and was built at the beginning of the 20th century. Franz Kafka worked as a clerk in the **Assicurazioni Generali Building** before attaining success as a writer. In this square, which has seen so many tragic events, the Czechs have repeatedly expressed their desire for freedom, often in a

The art nouveau architecture and interior of Central Station.

violent manner. In 1969, Jan Palach set fire to himself in protest against the Soviet occupation. The Velvet Revolution began here in 1989 when, taking advantage of the opportunity represented by the opening of the Berlin Wall, the Czechs finally threw off the yoke of totalitarianism. A monument to the victims of Communism recalls these painful episodes in the history of both city and country. Since the Velvet Revolution, this improvised memorial made up of crosses, wreaths, photographs and candles has stood under the watchful eye of St Wenceslas sitting astride his horse.

Statni opera Praha (Prague State Opera) is situated between the National Museum and Central Station. The building used to be known as the German Theatre but is now unofficially known as the Smetana Theatre.

The grand interior of the National Museum almost eclipses the collections which are exhibited in the galleries off this splendid staircase.

The pantheon of the National Museum (above) is decorated with paintings by Czech artists depicting great events in the history of the country.

The dome of the National Museum.

After the underground, the tram is the fastest way of getting around the city. Lines 14, 17 and 22 link the city's principal monuments.

The **National Museum** with its golden dome stands behind the statue of Wenceslas. Josef Schulz designed this spectacular building at a time when national pride was running high at the end of the 19th century. The visitor is able to discover many Czech national heroes depicted in the pantheon at the heart of this richly decorated building.

In addition to a library that is filled with ancient manuscripts, the National Museum also has natural history collections of fossils, animals and minerals. The visitor will also find archaeological and anthropological exhibits.

Imposing baroque statues attract the attention of even the most indifferent. This knotty tangle of limbs is complemented by the warmth and strength of the stone.

The altar of the Church of St Ignatius, dedicated to the founder of the Jesuit order.

Around Charles Square

In Prague, seats of learning are often set in the middle of greenery. Charles Square, with its grass, trees, flowerbeds and bubbling fountains is surrounded by the

The garden in Charles Square (left) is a green oasis in the middle of the largest square in Prague. It was included in Charles IV's urban planning scheme as a key commercial area and for a long time a cattle market was held there.

17th-century Jesuit college and the sober Czech University of Technology.

The infamous windows of Nove Mesto Town Hall.

The first and most terrible defenestration took place at Nove Mesto Town Hall in 1419 when supporters of the Hussite preacher Jan Zelivsky expressed their anger by pushing the Catholic consuls of Prague out of the window before finishing them off with their swords. And the reason for these drastic actions? The consuls had refused to free Hussite prisoners.

At the north end of Charles Square, in front of **Nove Mesto Town Hall**, there is a statue of Jan Zelivsky, responsible for the first defenestration of Prague in the 15th century. The **Church of St Ignatius** and the **Jesuit College** on Charles Square were both built in the 17th century by Lurago and Bayer. In 1773, the religious

The interior of St Ignatius's.

The baroque decor of the Church of St Ignatius was intended to inspire both the senses and the souls of the faithful.

On Resslova Street, the Czech University of Technology founded in 1867 has its premises in a splendid neo-Renaissance building.

order founded in 1534 by the Spaniard Ignatius of Loyola was dissolved and the Jesuit College was then transformed into a military hospital. It later became a teaching hospital and part of Charles University. On the other side of the square, the **Na Slovanech Monastery** was built in 1347 by Charles IV. Its two steeples were a much later addition.

It is said that in the Na Slovanech Monastery the devil assumed the guise of a cook in order to make the monks commit the cardinal sin of gluttony. When the cunning abbot discovered his plan, the devil changed himself into a cockerel. Unfortunately he did not have time to fly away before the monks had plucked him!

The ordinary looking building at 40 Charles Square stimulated the imagination of locals who christened it 'Faust House'. During the 16th century, it was occupied by an alchemist named Edward Kelley who was imprisoned by Rudolph II, probably because he had failed to change lead into gold. The facts of the story were quickly distorted by the inhabitants of Prague and Edward Kelley became Doctor Faust, killed by the devil.

The Church of St Cyril and St Methodius.

The Czech resistance workers who orchestrated the assassination of the German SS commander Heydrich, known as 'the hangman', took refuge in the crypt of the Church of St Cyril and St Methodius. Surrounded by the Nazis, the courageous Czechs chose to kill themselves rather than be taken alive.

On Resslova Street, the **Czech University of Technology**, founded in 1867, occupies a splendid neo-Renaissance building. A little further on, the baroque **Church of St Cyril and St Methodius** bears a plaque commemorating the tragic events which took place there during the Nazi occupation. Going back up Na Zderaze Street, in the direction of

The illuminated balconies of the National Theatre's imposing auditorium.

the **National Theatre**, a small detour via Kremenkova Street is a must for beer drinkers. U Fleku bar serves a delicious dark beer made on the premises which can be enjoyed in the garden or in the vaulted bar. After a little light refreshment, continue your walk in the direction of the fabulous neo-Renaissance National Theatre.

The National Theatre is a neo-Renaissance masterpiece that was funded to a large extent by donations. When it caught fire in 1881, just a few days after its opening, the people of Prague collected enough money to rebuild this symbol of national pride. Bedrich Smetana's opera Libuse was performed here to mark the reopening of the theatre two years later.

The elegant Masaryk Embankment is lined with attractive buildings.

As you walk back upstream along the Rassinovo and Masaryk Embankments, it is possible to take a trip on a cruise boat from one of the landing stages. Back on dry land, you can visit the museum dedicated to Anton Dvorak (1841–1904) in the Michna Summer Palace. The building is the work of Kilian Dientzenhofer and houses

Navigation on the Vltava is made possible by the little weirs built during the 19th century. These tiny waterfalls enable cruise boats to carry sightseers downstream. Drifting along with the swans, the passengers can view the riverside monuments from the Hanavsky Pavilion in the north to the cliff face of Vysehrad Rock in the south.

The Dvorak Museum.

The banks of the Vltava reflected in the calm waters of the river – a comforting sight for those who suffer from seasickness!

Bedrich Smetana, Jan Neruda, Alfons Mucha, Mikulas Ales and many others are buried in the artists' cemetery in Vysehrad.

the instruments and scores of the famous Czech composer as well as a photographic collection. To complete your tribute to this great musician, pay a visit to his tomb in the **Vysehrad cemetery**. Other famous people, such as Smetana, are buried in this cemetery which is entirely dedicated to important figures from Czech history.

The fortress of Vysehrad, to the south of Nove Mesto, was demolished in the 19th century during the period of national awakening and a cultural centre was erected in its place. The Slavin (or Pantheon) holds the remains of those individuals who have 'served their country well'.

Creative Workshop

Having discovered the wonders of Prague, it's now time to get creative.

All you need are a few odds and ends and a little ingenuity to keep the spirit of your adventure alive by creating your own beautiful craft objects.

These simple yet ingenious ideas capture the special flavour of Prague and leave you with a permanent reminder of your visit.

An original, simple and fun way to preserve your holiday memories.

Cat Panel

*T*his small wooden panel is inspired by Prague street signs and will make an attractive decoration for a door or child's chest of drawers.

Preparing the panel

• Rub down the wood with sandpaper and apply a first coat of white gesso or matt white acrylic paint.

• Allow to dry and sand down again.

• Continue painting and sanding until the grain of the wood is no longer visible.

• Paint the background with a wide paintbrush using very dilute Naples yellow, then dab the entire surface with a damp sponge to remove the brush marks.

• Apply two more coats, this time using yellow ochre followed by cadmium crimson or red ochre.

Painting the motif

• Copy the motif on tracing paper using a soft pencil and transfer it to the wooden panel.

• Paint the background (using a mixture of white, ultramarine and black) then the cats (white) and shaded areas (grey).
• Paint the curlicues around the cats starting at the lightest shadow and blend in, then apply red oxide or red ochre and blend in again.
• Paint the outer edges of the panel in the same way.
• Outline the cats in black and the curlicues in a mixture of red ochre and brown using a very fine brush.
• Apply a coat of gloss varnish and allow to dry before waxing the panel using a light wax to give it an 'antique' finish.

side (using a mixture of white and yellow ochre) and blend in the colour using a stencil brush.
• Apply pure yellow ochre to the areas which are to appear in

Materials

• a piece of plywood 1/4" (5mm) thick measuring approximately 8" x 12" (20cm x 30cm) • soft pencil • tracing paper • wide paintbrush • stencil brush • fine paintbrush • sponge • sand paper • pot of gesso or white matt acrylic paint • gloss varnish • light patina wax • acrylic paints in Naples yellow, yellow ochre, cadmium crimson or red ochre, brown, ultramarine, grey, white and black

Painted Eggs

The smooth rounded shape of eggs lends itself perfectly to the simplest of designs. Using traditional techniques, these everyday objects can be transformed into beautiful decorations.

Preparing the eggs

• Make a small hole at the top and bottom of each egg and blow out the yolk and white.
• Clean out with soapy water.
• Allow to dry.

Making a stand

• Before painting the eggs, make a stand out of plasticine by rolling it into a ring. The eggs can then be laid down or stood up on the ring, depending on the design.

Preparing the motifs

• On a sheet of paper, prepare a selection of different motifs.
• To ensure that the eggs go well together when finished, use all the colours on each egg.

Painting the eggs

• Choose colours that stand out well against the background.

• Paint the whole surface of the egg in a single colour and allow to dry.

• Paint a wavy line around the egg as shown.

• Decorate this line with dots, lines or circles in different colours. Allow time for each colour to dry.

• Decorate each side of the egg with a multi-coloured floral motif, using a different design for each egg.

Materials

• fresh eggs • plasticine • acrylic paint in white, red, black, yellow and orange • large paintbrush • fine paintbrushes

Decorated Glass Carafe

*I*t is very easy to etch designs on a plain glass carafe using etching paste. Here are some motifs to inspire you.

The stencils

• Create your own designs or copy these onto a wide strip of adhesive paper.
• Remember that the areas that you cut out of the stencil will be etched onto the carafe.
• Stick the stencil onto the carafe.

The etching

• Apply the etching paste over the stencil. Leave the paste to work for a few seconds.

The finishing touches

• Rinse the carafe under running water without removing the stencil.
• Wipe the stencil to remove surplus paste, remove the adhesive paper and clean using a sponge.

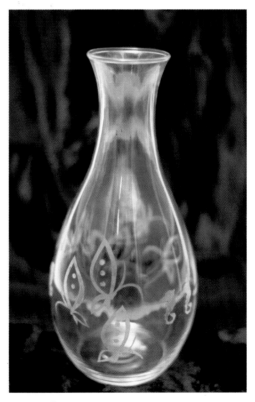

Materials

• carafe • etching paste • adhesive paper
• sponge

Mucha Stained-glass Panel

*M*ucha's art is timeless, featuring young girls with long wavy hair in a way that combines the natural with the geometrical. On stained glass, the light adds to the charm of these designs and brings them to life.

• If possible, choose a square design which is large enough to cover the piece of glass, or adjust the size using a photocopier.

• Clean the glass with white spirit and stick the design on the underside using sticky tape.

• When the lines need to be very fine, use a fine indelible marker instead.

• Once the outlines are dry, you can start painting using the glass paints.

separate the main blocks of colour.

• In some areas you will have to apply several coats to obtain the desired intensity of colour.

• To achieve the effect of shading, apply light brush strokes so that the colours only blend partially.

• First outline the design using the thick black marker: these lines make your painting look like a stained-glass window and

Materials

• a square of glass measuring approximately 8" x 8" (20cm x 20cm) • glass paint in yellow, red, green and black • thick black marker • fine indelible black marker • white spirit • sticky tape • paintbrushes

INDEX

Acknowledgements

The publishers would like to thank all those who have contributed
to the preparation of this book, in particular:

Angie Allison, David Bême, Antoine Caron, Jean-Jacques Carreras,
Aude Desmortiers, Nicolas Lemaire, Hervé Levano,
Mike Mayor, Kha Luan Pham, Vincent Pompougnac,
Marie-Laure Ungemuth, Emmanuèle Zumstein.

Creative Workshop:
Marie-Dominique Arignon (p. 132-133),
Céline Gerst et Rislane Lazrak (p. 136 à 139)

Translation: Sara Montgomery

Illustrations : Franz Rey, Valérie Zuber

Printed in Italy
Eurolitho – Milan
March 1999